NoH place Poetry

Anthology

Edited by
AJ Juarez, Julie Murkette & Stephen Campiglio

Lost Valley Press

Hardwick, Massachusetts

ISBN: 978-1-935874-43-0

Front Cover: Cyclical Man, circa 1906, by Raymond Duncan (1874-1966)

Back Cover: Untitled Woodcut, circa 1924, by Raymond Duncan

The front and back cover art were used with permission from Michel Duncan Merle and the Akademia Duncan.

Event Flyers: Bill O'Connell, Michel Duncan Merle, Charles Majka, Stephen Campiglio, and Richard Goulis

Book Design: Sarah Bennett
shbennettbookdesign.com

Dedicated to John Zaganiacz (1955–2022)
his amazing musicianship and goodwill
anchored the Noh Place Jazz Series
and his improvisations accompanied many other Noh events

Special Thanks
To the founders of Noh Place Artists Cooperative

To the City of Worcester
cradle of poetry and creativity for over a century

To Verna H. Urso, Stephen DiRado, and Warren Lehrer
for their assistance in locating the works of Esther Heggie,
Jacob Knight, and Brother Blue, respectively

To Shanee Stepakoff, Craig Semon, and Donna Juarez
for their editorial and content support

The Noh Place Poetry Anthology *has been a communal labor of*
love for all involved. The editors are very grateful to all the poets
who generously contributed their works.

Table of Contents

About this book

For more than a decade, Noh Place founder AJ Juarez considered the idea of compiling an anthology of the nearly 100 poets who participated in readings at Noh Place Artists Cooperative and its antecedent operation, Sea Otter Press (at Grove Street Gallery) from 1981 to 1996, including post-Noh Place years when the organization continued to sponsor events at other venues. We felt the variety and quality of the poetry that these events captured stood on their own merits and should be celebrated.

Juarez was reluctant, however, to embrace this project because he was concerned that it would elicit a longing for a Worcester scene that no longer existed. It is a challenge not to be nostalgic when the connecting tissue of an anthology is based on poetry readings that happened more than 30 years ago.

In an effort to avoid nostalgia and an aggrandizement of anyone's "glory days," while narrowing the selection of poets, we solicited work with the understanding that the poems may have been written before, during, or after the poets' participation in the Noh Place Poetry Series. Thus, the scope of this anthology spans decades, rather than presenting a "freeze frame" on time.

Each poet chose their own work for inclusion, and in the same spirit, wrote their own biographical statements, with the idea that such an approach would illustrate the variety of voices and experiences that were an essential component of Noh Place and its philosophy. We believe that this collection of poems, modified from its original, more inclusive plan, contains aesthetic value, poetic stylings, and/or socio-political relevance, and indeed, continues to stand on its own merits.

The participating seventeen poets in the anthology were chosen by Juarez for their local, regional, and/or national importance, and for their representation of the many styles and voices that exemplified the Noh Place Poetry Series. We regret that all of the poets who read for the Series over the years could not be included. This exclusion does not reflect any editorial bias or taste.

Five of the selected poets have passed away. We asked Noh Place founding member Stephen Campiglio to select their poems, write their biographical statements, and assist with reprint permissions. He is also one of the poets included in these pages. This book was designed by another selected poet, Sarah Bennett.

About Noh Place Artists Cooperative

Noh Place Artists Cooperative was founded on the premise that a group of artists interacting communally could break artificial barriers between artistic disciplines and encourage one another to experiment and collaborate. The founding members, AJ Juarez, Stephen Campiglio, Jonathan Blake, Michel Duncan Merle, Michael Lukaszevicz, Brian Jyringi, Charles Majka, and Jean Lozoraitis, all painters, musicians, and/or poets, provided the multidisciplinary and fertile ground for such an approach. The result was a performance/gallery space for art, music, poetry, theatre, open mics, workshops, and multimedia events, designed to welcome the public and serve as a collective member of its neighboring community. The Co-op's other incentive was to afford its founding members a place to exhibit and perform their own work.

On Saturday, March 7, 1987, Noh Place opened its doors at 117 Lovell Street in Worcester, Massachusetts, and began its comprehensive arts program of weekly events that would continue at this location through June of 1988. After this time, the Co-op went into hiatus for six months, while it sought a new place of operations.

Noh Place reopened in December of 1988 at 88 Webster Street in Worcester, organizing a fundraiser to help with the cost of renovating this new space, and resumed a program of weekly events in February of 1989. This second location, unfortunately, proved to be short-lived, and the programming continued only through July of that year, when Noh Place ceased to operate at Webster Street.

However, after nearly two years of organizing hundreds of events as a brick-and-mortar collective, the founding members became sponsors and participants of "Guerrilla Arts" programs into the 1990s, operating as Noh Place in Time or Noh Place Presents and staging shows at the Worcester Artist Group, Worcester State College's Blue Lounge, Applewild Day School in Fitchburg, and the QE2 in Albany, New York, shows that included the Solo/Duet Series, which received a grant from the Worcester Cultural Commission.

Noh Place exemplified an "open door policy," hosting both accomplished and beginning performers, and true to its original premise, fostered a communal spirit in which creative expression and collaboration were a prime focus. The Co-op's programs, advertised through its monthly calendar of events and disseminated through a mailing list of patrons and the Worcester media, included a weeknight poetry series, a Sunday jazz series, concerts and performances on Fridays and Saturdays, a gallery space for visual artists on a rotating schedule, and a variety of special events, all of which featured both local and nationally known artists.

As a 2021 *Worcester Telegram* article by Craig Semon about Noh Place states, "When it came to music, poetry, performance and visual art in the '80s, there was no place in Worcester like the relatively short-lived but culturally significant Noh Place Artists Cooperative."

Lost Valley Press
Hardwick, MA, 2022

Sarah Bennett always wanted to be a fiction writer but has no patience for big projects and gets too distracted by the small details. She was Poet Laureate of Worcester County in the 1980s and hosted the Poetry Beat on WCUW (91.3) for many years. If you went to the Coffee Kingdom during the mid-1980s, Bennett might have sat down uninvited at your table and recited poetry as part of the group "Poets on the Spot." She once performed at First Night Worcester as a pink poetry jukebox, complete with candy buttons. Bennett currently lives in Lynn, MA, where she works part-time as a book designer: shbennettbookdesign.com She has one full-length book of poems, *The Fisher Cat*, 2018.

These poems appeared in *The Fisher Cat*, Dytiscid Press, 2018, and are reprinted with permission from the author.

To the salamander who lives under my back step

You know how sometimes
in dreams

I am so pleased that my great great great
great grandmother is a salamander

you can fly
or talk to animals
or find the forest

And I am your cousin.
You have made a nice place here

full of candy? Well last night
I dreamed I was singing that magical song

under this rock for the past
350 million years.

and then you woke me and I have been trying all day
to sing it again.

To a Clear January

You slapped me
in the face
when I stepped out
your door, slapped my
face with your
diamond necklace
and my cheeks
burned bright

with joy. You
showed me world after
world, sun after sun
after sun. I was
thrilled to be so
cold, to suffer so
for my place
in heaven:
Zero Kelvin.

Turtle

My life is now divided into three parts.

I

Before, when I was happy.

II

The two seconds during which I saw the turtle
stick her head up out of the Miocene swamp and look
round at Route 62 in Maynard until

III

I returned too late to help her
cross the Modern Era.

The Mushroom

At that moment
in the middle of brown nowhere
we come upon the mushroom   a white bride

in pearly veil. We leap at her and
stagger back, knowing full well
the curse. She must be devised

of flesh, a lampshade alive
with reptilian warmth.
She could be nothing

but the destroying angel
Amanita, come to rid us
of autumn.

The Gold Thimble

For three days my 80-year-old mother looked
round and round for her mother's
thimble: small, bent, dimpled,
gold. "I know
I put it right here!" she wailed.

And then

she emptied a shoe worn the day before, and
the thimble sailed onto the counter,
declared itself found.

I'd like to do that:
reach down
and borrow what I used to wear
on the tip of my thumb
and then

return it, quietly,
like a ghost.

Jonathan Blake has been following the gospel of his heart for as long as he can remember. Writer, educator, arts activist/organizer, he makes his home in central Massachusetts. Currently he teaches in the English department at Worcester State University, where for the past 12 years he has hosted a round robin open reading series open to students, faculty and staff and the greater Worcester County poetry community called ONE POEM. His poems and essays can be found in an array of journals and anthologies, including *The Atlanta Review, Amoskeag, Brilliant Corners, Poetry East* and *The Worcester Review.* On occasion, he has had the privilege of fashioning his public readings in collaboration with some of the fine jazz musicians who also call central Massachusetts home.

Poems reprinted here with permission from the author.

Vigilance

My friend tells me he's been waiting
For days. Has painted nothing.
Each time I visit it is as if he has never moved,
Though he assures me his life continues:
Good harvest meals from his dying garden,
The simple pleasure of washing dishes,
Car repairs and unexpected phone calls,
Making slow love with his wife.
He tells me the waiting is necessary,
That the light moves with grace across
The small table where one branch of blossoms
Stands in the blue bottle, that he waits
For the petals to have just the right color
Of dying, that particular beauty
Of what will fall in its own sweet time.
How the spirit is revealed.
The decorative left behind.
He insists there is only one moment
Like this for each living thing.
That he must wait to paint the magnificence
In the moments after suffering.

Longing: Late Spring

— For Yuka

Rain begins again.
Birds build nests beneath the eaves.
How still my heart is.

Last night I stood above the pond
With a woman from Japan
Who said she knew how
Poems could be found here.
This morning she returned to Boston
And I am alone, only the moon
In memory as it climbed through
The hissing trees into a sky suddenly
Free of storm. Drinking cold wine
We said the names of Basho, Buson,
Issa like a prayer. We might have said
Crickets, night birds, shadows born
From a pale northern light.
Her small body swayed like a thin
Reed in the night breeze and she leaned
Closer to a moon older than any
Homeland either of us knows.

Yuka said —

The songs of birds at dusk are poems.
Moonlight does not break the grass.
I am far from home but in Japan
The sound of distant bells
Echoes in my heart.

THREE POETRY READINGS IN APRIL IN CELEBRATION OF
NATIONAL POETRY MONTH

April 11   Bill O'Connell / Kathy Gregg

April 18   Karen Hart / Stephen Campiglio

April 25   Jonathan Blake / Andre Juarez

Crocker Room ~ Applewild Day School
120 Prospect Street, Fitchburg, MA
Three Sundays @ 2:00 p.m.

A wine and cheese reception will follow each event. The readings are free and open to the public. For further information, please contact (978) 342-6808.

Letter to Elizabeth Away in France

I have wondered all day
What might be important enough to tell.
Certainly last night—the gray day growing darker
And me without sadness; at dusk
Two blue herons slow and prehistoric
Along the stillness at the center of the pond;
The haunting cry of doves.
And with morning—the world brilliant again,
Whispering what grows old in us:
Points of sunlight like diamonds spilled
Across water; one slow tractor turning
Yesterday's hay where the earth meets the sky;
Summer's wind lifting the heavy branches.
To know my heart now summon the smell of water
At dawn, the quiet voices of a father and son fishing
Among the fallen trees close to the far shore,
The sudden power of last night's rain.

In Praise of September

In the stillness of mid-morning
The man begins his meditation on loss,
Its weight in our lives, what can't
Be seen in the wind lifting
Lush branches of green that
Begin to burn toward autumn,
The old heart knowing September's tradition
Of sadness, the ghosts that whisper
Melancholy like the doves at dawn.

We must take measure of what is
Abundant as well, he thinks: The brightness
Of his wife's voice as she returns from errands
And walks into the kitchen; the smell
Of mint picked weeks ago now steeping
In hot water; the cold snap of metal
That signals letters from old friends
Who live close to the sea.

He sings quietly about the moon
Splintered by the dark
Pines in the early morning,
Shadows like ancient texts
He studied happily
On the bedroom wall
Before rising into the morning's
Slow bloom of light.

And harvest, he thinks. Two large
Blue bowls of ripe tomatoes.
Cut basil standing in the glass vase;
Cloves of garlic on the cutting board
Close to the shining knives. Coltrane's tenor
Floating through the warming rooms
Of late summer. And the work, he smiles,
Shaking his head, the work
That remains to be done.

NÕH PLAce

"I wonder whether Sonny Bono is having a good time tonight."

RUTH BOLTON BRAND ° ° ° ° ° ° ° ° ° °

AFTER THE SPAWN

We are flowing out to sea
        Our fins sparkle in the rapids
as we approach the dam
        We leave bits of scale on rock
Our jaws open to sunlight
        as it flicks down through
           clear water

Our clean vertebrae slip past
        salamanders and minnows
           that dart away
Our silver eggs lie in wait
        at the early spring of the river

plus ° ° ° ° O P E N   M I K E ° ° ° °
POETS, BRING NEW WORK TO SHARE...
5 minutes under the lights at

Noh Place Artist's Coop
corner of Maywood & Lovell, Worcester

THUR   APRIL 23rd   7:30 pm
parking in the rear behind the video store

Blue Miles

Not blue, but *"Kind of Blue"*
Was my heart in those early
Years on Castle Street, lying
On the broken couch in the bay
Window of my brick row house,
The music a new tenderness
I was discovering as the dirty
Light fell through the torn
And yellowed shades and the old man
In his garden of tomatoes across
The street whistled softly and wished
Good late afternoon to the junkies
Walking like the dead up
The street to the park where
They would fix, nod on the grass
Under the unblemished blue
Of Worcester, sunlight warming
Their gray faces, lighting their dreams
Before an indigo blue held
A bright rising moon over
The darkening tenements
And Miles' muted trumpet
Whispered into a breathless
Stillness, and even love,
Even love seemed possible.

Ruth Bolton Brand was an actress, puppeteer, painter and costumed historian, who loved playing an old organ in candlelight and making pastel portraits of fellow workers, wrote poetry, fiction and drama—her play *Farmer Took a Wife* was staged twice. She once designed a house and did the carpentry work. Her writing appeared in Amherst's *Peregrine, Sahara,* and *The Worcester Review,* winning two poetry awards. Her book, *Heart Pound,* of 25 short stories, was published by Xlibris. She created illustrated chapbooks of her work and self-published *Trails, Trysts & Twists,* a bi-polar memoir of her world travels. She had two sons, eight grandchildren, four great-granddaughters and a black cat.

Poems reprinted here with prior permission from the author.

Editors Note: Sadly, Ruth Bolton Brand passed away on April 17, 2022, before Noh Place Poetry Anthology *was published.*

Swampland

He waits at the gate with bramble arms,
tiger lilies shimmy up, entangle us
in tight embrace. Our initials carve
valentines on a circular stump.

We freeze beneath the moon, mists and water
run past. I stumble across chasms, over rocks
and stone, tumble into fists of barbed wire,
plunge into quicksand. My hair streams,

my nose quivers, my knees knock, I gnash
my teeth, splash through purple grapes,
lavender baths of ginseng tea. I carry rice
cakes and olive oil to our feast.

Woods

If I stay out of the woods
I'll be safe. The words dissolve
on my teeth, stick in my throat.

If I keep completely away,
don't gaze into deep caverns
of pine tree groan, needle prick,

long-stemmed mushrooms,
never again explore avenues
of trailing arbutus, taste

wintergreen, succumb to earth
root hammock, pitch trickling
down my neck, leaves crunching

under my buttocks, my heart
chewed by wolves staring out
of my own eyes. If I sit on a

three-legged stool in my square
prison with only a tiny window
floating a feather of imagination,

if I stay wrapped in my own
tree branch limbs, vine leaf
hair, lace fern dress, part of

the overall plan of wolves
is that I be swept back
by a broom into the woods.

Silhouette

Although she lies below, she rises above,
her spirit flies to trees, to sky, to clouds,
rain and rainbows.

A black Halloween cat, she yowls at
midnight, serenading witches and hobgoblins,
at dawn she slides back

into her hole, until darkness pulls her out
again to howl sounds against the moon.
Her ghost is there scaring

pumpkins piled in fields of yellow corn,
I see her and remember but never
shudder at her sight.

Sky Eyes

A vast wet green earth map
leads to an ice ballet of blue peaks,
    church spires offer saints
and gargoyles to murky sky.
Glacial triangles intersect marble
    blue-purple mountains, lightning rods,
pastures thick with green weeds,
daisies, buttercups. Crooked limbs
    drip apple blossom clouds, a pair
of orange mums lie sleep-wrapped
together with graven eyes.

Brother Blue, the stage and performance name for Hugh Morgan Hill, was a storyteller, educator, actor, musician, and street performer, based mostly in the Boston area. After serving in the segregated US Army in World War II, he earned a BA from Harvard University in Social Relations, an MFA from the Yale School of Drama, and a PhD in Divinity (with a concentration in pastoral sacred storytelling) from the Union Institute in Cincinnati, delivering his doctoral presentation at Boston's Deer Island Prison, accompanied by a 25-piece jazz orchestra. Brother Blue performed frequently and widely throughout the country at storytelling festivals and also abroad in England, Russia, and the Bahamas, but was, perhaps first and foremost, a regular performer on the streets of Boston and Cambridge, most notably in Harvard Square. In 2009, he was awarded the W.E.B. Du Bois Medal from the Du Bois Institute at Harvard, which was accepted posthumously on his behalf by his spouse Ruth Edmonds Hill. He died in Cambridge in 2009 at the age of 88.

Brother Blue performed at Noh Place in April 1988 and July 1989.

---

you and me

for ruth

i make a joke
you think of something sad
an eagle is afraid of heights
don't be afraid
so what if you fall
just fall
fall into the stars
into the meadow

i throw away words
your head pumps blood throughout your body
i'm on fire!
you say
what are you gonna do with it now?
i say
give it all away
for free

you say
what!

i say
nothing
i don't want nothing in return

you fall in love with the sidewalks
i fall in love with the trees
i close my eyes and see flying polka-dot elephants
and hear the giraffes sing about the wildebeest and the unicorn

we did this all before
before before ago
somewhere
we rehearsed this thing eons ago
that's how come it be so tight
but watch out
there are wolves around
just watching the streets
looking for unsuspecting lambs to eat

i whisper one word in your ear and fall over
you turn the page and say
the superstars are all around

i say you're right
could be some guy
he's an old guy
he bags groceries
could be the street sweeper
the keeper of the flame
(the one with no name)
could be an acrobat
the old lady sleeping under a box on the corner

it could be the person the next door down
come to think of it
it could be you

you tell me i'm mad
we laugh together

the sound of a train passes through the window
the room shakes
my left hand falls asleep
the moon pops out from behind a cloud
promising another morning
together with you

a few good books

the problem is
there are so many books to read
how can anyone get to all of them?

well
if you're lucky
you marry someone who works in a library
that way you can marry every book on the shelf
each one saying
help yourself
(that's what i did)

a cool book

this is a cool book
the first thing you do when you see this book is take off all your
clothes
and run around
then you fan yourself with the pages
the book is cool
very physical

people look at you funny with this book
but what the hell
it's cool
it's a cool book

lots of things

you open this book like a purse
it's called lots of things
but it's got nothing in it

a little nothing

one of the great things about this book is
you expect nothing
you open it up to see what nothing looks like
and it erupts
it's got all kinds of things in there
marbles and buttons
soda caps
the smell of pizza
all kinds of things

clemency

a horseshoe lands in a prison cell
it sprouts golden wings
the thing can fly!

(it's taken away from the inmate
gets sold to a major publisher
becomes a best seller
and is hailed as a masterpiece
the only thing is
it's not allowed in prison)

the living thing

one day god shook his head and thought
what a drag what they done to the word
scriptures turn into shields
spears of holy terror
waging war with words
all these words
people killing people over books
over words in books
they burn the books!
they've fallen under a spell
it's called
the idolatry of the printed word
it's time to try something new

the next day
god makes a new kind of book
in it is what no book ever had:
the living thing
it's a wordless book
it glows
it's full of light

it appears one night in a child's crib
the child picks it up and says
aaahhhhh
she opens it up and hears laughter
she turns the page and hears a tear drop

it's all in there

next
the book winds up in a mental hospital
this old man has been in there fifty years
he looks at the book
he doesn't know how it got there
he opens it up
he laughs
he cries at the same time

in the winter time
roses come to the book
he takes a whiff
aaahhhhh
cover to cover
the book is full of life

right now a blind man's got it
he's carrying it with him
he can hear the sound of thunder
and see lightning too
he reads it with his fingers and toes

somebody asks what's the name of the book?

you can't name it

yeah but it's got to have a name

okay okay
the name of the book is

_____

unutterable

when you open the front cover it's like opening a window
everything is there
it's every book there ever was
it's microscopic
it's the size of your mind

well
word got out about this book
(hard to keep something like that a secret)
and now everybody wants a copy
but you can't find it in the local bookstore or library
this book finds you

<u>tomb book</u>

when i die
hope they bury me in a library
wish they could put me in a book someplace
some child open that book
a tear of happiness
rolling down his face

inside of me

when i look in the mirror
i see a lot of people
i see my grandfather on my father's side
he was born a slave
i see his father
his father was a white man
he was a master
(i'm not going to say his name)
he killed his own daughter
he wanted to father more light-skinned slave children
he just walked into the slave quarters one night
and tried to take his daughter
like he took her mother
but she wouldn't sleep with him
so he killed her
right there in bed

what happened?

nothing
he just rode off on his horse
it's in my blood
the killer's in me
there's a white man in me
riding off on a horse somewhere

i visited those slave quarters down in alabama
the family is still there!

my great-grandfather was a southern aristocrat
i guess underneath all these rags
i got a little bit of that aristocrat slave master

but you know who's also inside of me?
a black man from africa
selling off his brothers and sisters to slavery
that's some heavy stuff inside me too
some kind of screaming blues
they sold their own brethren!

i tell you
sometimes i feel a rage come from way down deep
and i say
hey man
you helped sell your brothers and sisters to white people
you shouldn't have done it!
why'd you do it?
i'm angry with you
you cooperated with these people
you helped to break your own
they tamed us like you tame a beast
you helped them put us in chains
you betrayed your own blood
that's how white people got away with that shit
you helped them all over the world
people of color adored white people
that's what happened in india

indonesia
australia
all over the americas
they came off of those big boats
and we adored these white people like they were angels
they had all these beautiful things
we thought they were gods!
we bowed down
we cooperated
oh africa
why did we do it?

same thing in this country today
blacks are killing each other
i can't even turn on the t.v.
white folks like to report on that stuff
you notice?
they call it *black on black violence*
it keeps them feeling like they're still our masters

people often ask
why you raise your voice like that?
why you so violent?
why this killing?
why this anger?

can't you see?
there's a battle raging

AT

NÕH PLACE

BROTHER BLUE

BROTHER B L U E ∘∘∘∘∘∘∘∘∘∘∘∘∘∘∘∘∘

brother blue brother
blue brother blue
brother blue brother
blue brother blue
brother blue brother
blue brother blue
brother blue brother
blue brother blue
brother blue brother
blue brother blue
brother blue brother
blue brother blue
brother blue brother
blue brother blue
brother
blue!!!

B
B
R
O
T
H
E
R

B
L
U
E
∘

Brother Blue has traveled around the globe as a master of storytelling, enchanting his audience with "meta-jazz" for over a generation. He is a survivor straight from Shakespearian times, his court being the street.

This concert/performance will be in collaboration with TRASHART, a multi-media group which emphasizes spontaneity and intuitive, electro-human-jam-session-like new music.

Donation: $5.50

Saturday   July 22nd   9pm

Noh Place Artists Cooperative
88 Webster St. (4th Floor in the rear) WORCESTER

there's some howling blues
silent blues
every time i point a finger
there's a finger pointing right back at me
because inside of me
i got two black men wrestling with each other
and a white man watching the whole thing from the wings
then the white man fights with one of the black men
while the other black man stands there watching
now they're all fighting each other inside of me
trying to kill one another
trying to kill me!

there's another couple of people in there too
trying to keep the peace
they're in there
all these men
they're trying to kill me
they're trying to keep from killing
they're wrestling with each other
they're trying to keep the peace

During his involvement with Noh Place, Stephen Campiglio was also a member of the weekly improvisational collective, Forbidden Poets, whose performances aired live on many Sunday nights in the late 1980s on WCUW 91.3 FM in Worcester. He later founded and directed the poetry series at Borders Book Shop in Framingham, MA and the D'Alzon Arts Series at Assumption College, and then in 2006, founded and directed the Mishi-maya-gat Spoken Word & Music Series at Manchester Community College in CT, a series that would run for 12 years. His poetry and translations have recently appeared in *Aji, Chiron Review, Circumference (Pi Poetry), DASH, Glimpse, Journal of Italian Translation, Miramar, Pensive, Pinyon Review, Sangam Literary Review, Stand* (Leeds, England), *VIA: Voices in Italian Americana, The Wayfarer, Wild Roof Journal,* and *Woven Tale Press Magazine.* Winner of the Willis Barnstone Translation Prize for a poem by Giuseppe Bonaviri (1924-2009), Campiglio has now completed a manuscript of selected Bonaviri translations entitled *The Ringing Bones.* His current project, with co-translator Elena Borelli, will result in the complete translation of Giovanni Pascoli's (1855-1912) volume of poems, *Canti di Castelvecchio.* Twice-nominated for a Pushcart Prize, he was a quarterfinalist in the 2018 Codhill Press contest for a book-length manuscript and has published two chapbooks, *Cross-Fluence* (2012) and *Verbal Clouds through Various Magritte Skies* (2014).

"Bite to Eat" first appeared in the chapbook, *Cross-Fluence* (Soft Spur Press, Missoula, MT: 2012). The other poems reprinted with permission from the author.

Bite to Eat

— after Max Ernst

In a café that has remained open despite construction and the smell of paint and plaster, customers are passing around menus. Each collage-like card is unique; proof that the chef is some sort of wizard. Although there isn't any food on the tables, nor visible wait staff, the act of meditating on the art seems to stir the customers into other forms of satiation. I take a seat at the counter, and while waiting for a menu, make a rubbing of the wood-grained top with my napkin and pencil where the faces to my left and right magically appear in the frottage. But when I look up, they're phantoms, and my surroundings, now a studio space, belonging to Max Ernst. His trademark "sun-and-moon eclipse" adorns the transom. Works in various stages crowd the corners. On a shelf there's a monograph of the artist, and I open to:

. . . makes a Rhineland forest out of the edges of wallpaper . . .

I repeat these words aloud until the phrase achieves the power of an incantation, and Ernst steps out from behind an easel where the decalcomania of a forest on the canvas is still wet. Then handing me his latest collage, he explains that it's assembled like a menu, with the illustrations depicting his appetite for a variety of artistic techniques. The text and images serve as ingredients for the vessel of my body that begins to function alembic-like. Heated by the divine, I rise and fall, One with All. This must be one of those forms of satiation, I think. In the process, the master metamorphoses into a phantom, and I'm counter-side in the café again, passing my menu onto the next customer.

Row House

Kneeling beside the recliner
I just hurled from my third floor porch
a few minutes before,
I intone into its busted side
a plea for forgiveness.
Then embracing my new-found predicament,
I hug the bulk of the thing,
and reflect on the continuing tale of Castle Street,
now listed in the National Register of Historic Places.
When this row house was built in 1873,
it abutted the grounds of Oread Collegiate Institute
up there on Goat Hill.
The castle-like structure,
erected with stone quarried right from the hillside,
was the first all-women's college in the country.
Its founder, Eli Thayer, a man of classical erudition,
took its name from the mountain nymphs of Greek lore,
and renamed the slope Mount Oread.
Castle Park has since replaced the razed building,
but Oread continues to exist, as eternal as myth,
as plainly evident as the photographs of it that exist.
Still here on my knees in the gravelly end of the street,
I implore the Institute's disassembled towers
to rise again above the wooded ledge
and offer me the view that residents
must've seen decades ago.

And I believe that the nymphs themselves
have empowered this speculative moment.
As it begins to rain, I get up and sink
into the remains of the recliner:
a jumble of springs, limbs, and destinies,
converging into one body's angelic decline.

Sonorous Dream

— after Giuseppe Bonaviri

Returning to his hometown after his death
along the psychic remains of memory,
Giuseppe fills the narrow streets,
pauses at the open squares,
draws deeply from the hilltop air,
and prays for the blessing of Saint Agrippina,
before pressing on to the nearby plateau of Camuti,
where the prickly pear
oscillates in a curl of magnetic waves.

Beside the Rock of Poetry, in stark solitude,
his face exuding the leathery sheen of olive leaves,
he hears the murmuring of poems
by farmers, bakers, tailors, and shoemakers;
each in turn, populating his pliant mind.

When the concatenate sound
of his elders dies down,
he intones his own hymn
to star-fed fields of fava beans,
the dense crowns of carob trees,
breezes scented with donkey dung,
the native and migrating birds of the region,
violet mountains, baskets of snails,
almond buds bursting into bloom,
vermillion skies, the moon inside a seashell . . .

until a cold gust exacts from him further change
and he's overcome by a trembling crescendo
that peaks and upon whose diminishing shoulders
he exits into dark, silent infinity,
leaving me with the sonorous moment of his voice.

Address in the Underworld

City trash a foot deep inches along,
as if with many feet;
the bulk of refuse, having long overwhelmed
the capacity of the earth.

A hand inside of me tugs at the root of my brain.
The other hand tries the lock on a door in vain,
then another, and several more,
but for what or to see whom, I'm not sure.

Now entertaining the sick thought that the globe's
been infested by two-legged rodents
and that I'm one of them, isolated from the pack,

I prick my nose to the wind,
follow the smell of the subway,
wafting up to the street,
and take the stairs down to the station,
but for which train or to go where, I'm not sure.

Waiting on the platform for such a timeless stretch,
I lose track of whether it's day or night
or which city I'm in.

At last, from the dark mouth of the tunnel,
the tongue of a train issues forth,
but to say or demand what I'm not sure.

All I can say with certainty is that
when the doors open, I'll take a seat
and remain there until this poem's complete.

The Crows of Castle Hill

Asleep, I turn on my side,
while the roost occupies the hill outside.
Having gathered quietly in the trees,
they then maneuver among themselves
without a sound.

My arm, extending into the dark,
protrudes over the slope
like one of the branches;
fingers reaching the opposite ledge.

After a few birds land on me and leave,
I draw my hand to my nose
for an intimate scent of these gathering crows.

Nearly every corner of the earth hosts its own species,
which makes me wonder, from the hillside of my dream,
if the oneiric world boasts a variety of *Corvus*.

These birds may have crossed the mythic divide
as divine messengers of Apollo's oracle,
or as descendants of their two prototypes,
"thought" and "memory,"
once perched on the shoulders of a creation deity.

When dawn comes, the silence takes a dissonant turn,
waking subsumes the dream,
and the roost launches an aural assault on the human ear,
blaring from the hill a diatribe of the injustice
they've suffered through misperception.

Often mistakenly viewed as undesirable creatures
by contemporary cultures, and killed for centuries,
crows have proved to be more clever than their persecutors,
and also withhold their song.

Christopher Gilbert was born in Birmingham, Alabama, in 1949, and grew up in Lansing, Michigan. He earned two degrees in psychology: a BA from the University of Michigan and an MA from Clark University; 1972 and 1975, respectively. In 1977 Gilbert co-founded, with Etheridge Knight, the Worcester Free People's Artist Workshop, and was also active for many years in the Worcester County Poetry Association. A recipient of two fellowships from the Massachusetts Artists Foundation, he earned a poetry fellowship from the National Endowment for the Arts in 1986. His first book, *Across the Mutual Landscape*, won the 1983 Walt Whitman Award from the Academy of American Poets, and was published in 1984 by Graywolf Press. He was Poet-in-Residence at the Robert Frost Place in Franconia, New Hampshire in 1986, and served as the editor of the anthology, *Something Else: A Sample of Writing from Third World Writers*, published by *Dark Horse Magazine* in 1981. His poems and essays have been published in numerous magazines and in several anthologies, including *The Morrow Anthology of Younger American Poets* and *The Jazz Poetry Anthology*. His poem, "Any Good Throat," is installed in granite at the Jackson Square stop of the Boston MBTA subway system.

Gilbert worked as a psychotherapist in a variety of settings, including the University of Massachusetts Medical School Counseling Center, the Judge Baker Guidance Center, and Cambridge Family and Children's Service, in addition to teaching writing classes at Goddard College, Worcester Poly-technic Institute, University of Pittsburgh, Trinity College, and Clark University. He began teaching psychology at Bristol Community College in Fall River in 1993, a position that he held for the remainder of his life. After a twenty-year battle against the complications of polycystic kidney disease, Gilbert died in 2007.

The Backyard
from *Horizontal Cosmology*

Suddenly this voice is calling
when I go to the backyard.
The garden leaves cut the wind to singing
and their bodies, the perfect green
instruments for what they do.

The tree next door whose leaves
are phrases falling
where the wind is blowing,
the arpeggio of the Charlie Parker tune—
and impossible flight of notes.
And I'm humming to myself.

I will work the day out here, singing.
It makes me a gift with myself.
Something to make the yard bigger.
My hands fall at my sides, octaves apart.
How far? Clear enough for my friends
who look for me to feel between them.

Turning into Dwelling

Lord, am I ready? The crickets' sonic party clicks
deep in the grass outside in same tired dying tick
meting out a statistic that does not jump the awful gap
of now. The edge of the window is a groove
that the wind quivers through, making a music—
each note death or a map of destiny.
The midnight is a limit past which I must reach. Invite me
to be part of it. I will not wake and not sleep
unless I can be the language that is this time, words
which risk enough to read and sing to let me come to be
the unmapped footsteps of this summer night come down.

Everything is before me now. It arises all the way
from the walk from the sea to the last sound said
in my tongue. As another seed in which
the most forsaken responsibilities rise up assuming
a place—West Africa, Black Alabama, anthems
of the rueful survivals of the urban Midwest, all
the clotted truths in my blood are loud with those throngs.
The hopes and fears of the screen door's clack in the wind
are a calendar with pages as real as the clock's
click. I turn them to the cadence of the mission
my father left me tucked in the nut in his heart.

The dark July night is a fluid spreading
throughout every minute of me. It is my continuity.
But ghosts are always out there, Lord.
The newspapers are filled with tales of those more
ripe than me who are frozen as a passing note in history—
knives, gunfights, the viruses of fate itself, everywhere
the evidence of this inescapable disease that leaves
the temporary survivor wailing on his hardened knees.
I have made it to my early middle age. The duty
that you have passed to me at every page
is to get those dead into my life, and then defy them.

Now the weariness of race, not the transcendental tears,
now the Black man's blues and booze and reeling with a fate
so fucking hard you're best to sometimes shuck it,
now the thrown-up hands and the laugh about everything,
and the flight from it all with a faith that takes on nothing—
Hellhound on my behind, catch me further on down the line.
Statistical bullets in the air, hide my soul away in prayer.
Lord, the anguish of my Black block rises up in me
like a grief. My only chance to go beyond being breach—
to resist being quelled as a bit of inner-city entropy—
is to speak up for the public which has birthed me.
To build this language house. To make this case. Create.
This loving which lives outside time. Lord, this is time.

Blue

Everyone is gone. Everyone.
At a gutted store building
in his old neighborhood
Willie idles, kicking the rubbish.
By chance the odd pieces gather
into a stick figure—a boy.
Willie adds bits of cloth
and an old mop head for hair,
but he finds no object to be
a word to coax his boy to talk.
The face is a cracked white plate.
Willie throws it to the road
hoping a tire explodes.
The image exists when it confirms
our sense of being. Willie feels blue
like the sky, so close so far away.
When he opens his mouth
there is no sound but a window.
He opens it wide to show more air.

Charge

Gimme the ball, Willie is saying
throughout this 2-on-2 pick-up game.
Winners are the ones who play, being
at the sidelines is ridiculous.
So what happens here is a history
won not by the measure of points,
but by simply getting into it.
Willie plays like it could all be gone
at once, like his being is at stake.
Gimme the ball, he cusses.
Gwen Brooks's player from the streets.
The game is wherever there's a chance.
It is nothing easy he's after,
but the rapture gained with presence.
His catalogue of moves represents
his life. Recognize its stance.
So alive to be the steps
in whose mind the symbol forms,
miraculous to be the feeling
which threads these steps to dance.
The other side is very serious—
they want to play him 2-on-1.
Messrs. Death and Uniformity.
He's got a move to make them smile.
Gimme the ball, Willie says again
and again, *Gimme the goddamn ball.*

Glimpses

Up the hillside beyond the road's
dirt edge the evening comes and the harvest
air holds the sun's warmth in a last burning
breath hanging overhead a fever to the sky.
Valley drifts towards the end of blue,
my dogs lose their selves with skunk stink,
wag their lives on squirrels' fat tracks.
A couple in the east walking Vermont in a spell,
finding a circling road which they pursue
forward as though they might be late. Moon
clears a tree blocking out horizon,
rose red swollen outside its distance.

Suddenly, as if some hold had broken,
the leaves fall one and then another
from that maple, like fires flickering downward
and, the moon sighs bigger than its mouth.
Hearing an animal's proud body ease
in the grass, I turn to my friend
whose face floats below a layer of sweat—
a light clay pot where juice flows over.
Her eyes reflect the wave of wind
through a field of hazel grain, and me
the beaming farmer knowing it is time.

Chosen to Be Water

Across the field the great willow rocking its head
back and forth in the waters of the wind
might mean a hard storm, but who notices?
Suddenly the rain against the westward windows
arrives hard, but honest enough to dictate
the season. Bob Marley is dead today, and
the woman's neighbor aims the bass in his stereo
to match the raindrops' episodic flaring—
but not the dark explosions where they strike
the glass, and not the lament this acid will
etch into the garden which collects it.
She imagines a cabbage out there,
wet, standing against the moist black ground
like a pimple glistening or else a teardrop.
A leaf breaks from it, joining the spill
washed down between rows, and she says, *teardrop.*
Right now the chip on her shoulder is so sharp
she has no need to be disinterested
in pursuing the simile further, as the leaf
flows slowly downhill towards a gully.
She says the fallen leaf is a tear, too.
Suddenly she swears and shakes a sweat off—
squeezes her hips hard while she hums a song.
She wants the bold stroke of intense change.
Music has chosen to be water again.
Is it raining in her neighbor's apartment?
She will go see, and pushes herself up
from a table already wet with her judgment.

Esther Heggie was born in 1943 in Rutland, Vermont, and attended the Burr and Burton Academy in Manchester, Vermont. In her late teens, her family moved from Vermont to Boston, where she met and married Vernon Heggie. Esther and Vernon had three daughters, Verna, Doris and Claire. Later in life, she had grandchildren, Chay, Jarred, Nick, Amanda, and Matthew, and twelve great-grandchildren, all of whom she adored. After losing her husband in 1979, Esther decided to continue with her studies in English literature, poetry, and women's studies at Worcester State College and Clark University. Over the years, she performed her poetry at Noh Place, Grove Street Gallery, Worcester State College Poetry Center, and many other venues in the Worcester/Boston/Florida area, and also made appearances on radio shows, including at WCUW in the 1980s and 90s. Esther published several books during her career as a poet and performer (often publishing under the name of Fire): *Vermont/Paris Odyssey, Wolf Nights, Sensual Rhythms & Purple Bats* (with Virginia Rubino), *Sancara Gold*, and *Liquid Lovers*. She also published in the *Charlton Poets & Friends Books I and II*, as well as many other publications. In her later years, Esther settled in Maryland, where she continued to participate in poetry groups. She also spent a great deal of time engaging the imaginations of her great-grandchildren with her many stories. In 2018, Esther became ill and passed away, surrounded by family and friends.

Reprinted with permission from the Esther Heggie Estate, Verna H. Urso, executor.

My Emily Dickinson poem

Life got stuck
    in pain's way
Death
    Again closed
    The door

Country Poetry

Simply
The smell of just cut hay
On a warm summer Breeze
A meadow full of cows,
And I am young again!

Poets without Privilege

Poets without privilege
Without homes
Walk the streets
Trying to get enough to eat.

Little red jar

boy of the apache/ iroquois face

Jarred/my little darling
We met long ago
In a mystical unity
& we will always be together
Across time
As you grow
 & know love

You are all races
& you will share freedom
 With all peoples

You must walk barefoot
 In the sand
 In the soil

Wherever the mother goddess
 Flows to freely
In water/fire & sky

& I will be there
To love you
As you love your sisters

& we will plant flowers
 In the forever

Untitled

I will wait for you
In another place—
Another lifetime—
And an endless eternity
Will guarantee the perfection
That was not allowed
In this lifetime

Leaving Worcester

Cora walked out onto the porch/
Into the cool night air
She felt like a stranger
Observing the night
A street of three deckers
Who observed her?
An asphalt night
But you could still hear
The crickets
A porch two stories high
Not a porch that led to earth
To that from which compounded
Our beings
But a porch that could be left only by floating
Flying or falling
An escape square
That extended five spaces
Into a possibility
Cora sat/breathed/observed
felt/freedom call her
To the water/ to the willow
To the red clay

A Tennessee Williams/street car named
magnolia/sweet-bird of youth night
Fans waving/swaying/ice cubes
            Clinking

Throat-swallowing night
A Truman Capote/ Aunt Emily/ William Faulkner
                night/
A Swanee river/ Mississippi River
And the yahoo uniting their flow
To the delta/flooding bottom-land
                Crops night/
rice/ chicken/ okra/ red beans
And crawfish steaming
On a pot-bellied stove
In a bayou shack night
A Carson McCullers piano-playing
                night/
Cora rose and left this small
New England city of strangers/
A city built for European entry-way
For factory production
For pseudo-intellectuals
Cora rode a steamboat from
St. Louis down the quarter alone
With a mint julep in one hand
& bonbons
In the other

AJ Juarez is of the Ashiwee and Yeomen First Nations (Zuni and Yaqui). He is a poet, artist, writer, and musician. He is the founder of Noh Place Artists Cooperative and the former lead singer for The Ghost Shadows, a seminal Worcester musical experience known for its unusual blending of jazz, heavy metal, funk, Native American songs, and straight ahead rock. His Native flute musings can be heard on John Zaganiacz's *Virtual Equinox* recordings.

As a student he coordinated the Poetry Center at Worcester State College and was a founding member of The Center for the Study of Human Rights. He was deeply involved in the No Nukes and Anti-Apartheid movements. He is a lifelong Jazz aficionado and a former Jazz host at WCUW (91.3 FM). His Jazz poetry and artwork can be seen on the jazzhistorydatabase.com website. His art work has also been used on book covers and as illustrations. In the 2018 exhibition, "A Forty Year Retrospective" at the MAP Gallery in Easthampton, MA, AJ and his visual arts mentor, Michel Duncan Merle, highlighted their collaboration as artists and poets.

AJ lives on a lake in Western Massachusetts. He is the Managing General Partner at Ready Electronic Data Interchange and Associates, an information technology company working in Public Health.

Poems reprinted with permission from the author.

Why Not Ask Questions?

— for Leonard Peltier

Are those voices we are hearing   manic
Quetzal screaming
for us to save the Ozone?

The cry I bring back from the mountain,

can it be recycled?

Why not ask questions,
It's not about fear?

An ode to those who question

— *For my mother and our Ashiwee (ZUNI) roots for she taught me to question.*
— *For Stephen Hawking, whose book* A Brief History of Time, *reminded me of the importance of questioning.*

I

The sky is clear and the moon is crescent.
A hot summer wind blows.
I've come to sit alone, to clear my mind
of thoughts which spin and weave,
shuffle and stray,
and say nothing.

I think of the billions of stars, out there,
in the known universe. My mind is fragmented
and fills its self with thoughts of Mayan Astronomers and
inter-stellar voyages of the Zapotec.
Thoughts of Newton's discovery of the spectrum of color found
in a prism, of Hubble's notion of the expanding universe,
of Einstein—that Zionist gift to humanity. My thoughts
boil and steam, clatter and squeak until the image of
Stephen Hawking appears.
Professor Hawking,
sitting in his wheelchair, deformed, pained, struggling with
speech, exploring, searching, living his life,
writing, his *A Brief History of Time.*
His life full of meaning and significance,
celebrating questioning,
becoming

part of the continuum covering the globe we call earth
kin to the Chinese and their knowledge of rocketry
and to those Arabic thinkers who gave us
those powerful numerals we count.
Hawking, contributing; challenging; powerful.

The clear sky leads me towards
the desert horizon, I've often called home.
I walk towards the horizon,
"My mother is dead, she taught me to question,"
I say to the stars as I tip an imaginary hat
to those who have asked,
"How does it work, this universe of ours?"

II

This clear windy night humbles me.
I, a grieving man in awe with creation.
I raise my hands to the cosmos
and cry.

Pablo

— For the Chilote and Mapuche people

Pablo// Neftali, YOU POET,
GHOST-MENTOR,
lover of creation, you!
Have you re-incarnated as a leopard
or an olive tree?

Is there another common denominator—
besides DNA—
between your killers and the oranges
you loved?
Isn't CHILE
a delicious name for a country?

Questions For Catholics

Does confession absolve a Catholic Priest
Of pedophilia?
Why is the nun so threatened by my question?

Does the POPE know
The joy of a tender kiss after making love?

IF

— To Weezie

If, somehow, I could paint your laughter,
I would use yellows and pinks to illustrate your
Thundering belly.
Lavender and oranges, with a bit of white, for
The pure joy seeded in your womb.
    Your laughter would pass through bright desert yellows,
        sprinkled
With a bit of turquoise and black,
Making its way to the thorax, to
Burst through
Vocal chords of pastel rainbows, with a tingling sensation,
Which would stay in a passion red mouth,
Long after the echoes
Of your song
Had died.

Then your eyes would shine with
Clear kindness.

Bolonica—The Dancer

— for Jen

Your feet
Somehow hold up the cosmos
Because *en pointe*
Balance becomes a living-breathing demigod,
A glorious moment dedicated to integrity
And space.

Your legs hold up the moment as an offering
To unknown gods who
Demand perfection and years of practice
And blood sacrifice.

Your torso and waist are sweet rain
Nourishing a rain forest as they move
Gracefully like a comet or a swimming polar bear
Giving us reasons to gasp in amazement
And briefly rejoice with you
In the glow of a grand performance sprinkled with a
shimmering   charisma.

Your arms and hands point towards heaven on earth,
And to the possibility of strength and sensitivity.
They are a conduit to all gods who are proud and
Even astonished by their creations.
You are a song of reverence and delight.

Your face is the breath of life
And its incandescence.

On leaving Boston (I–90 West)

We routinely part the ether with fossil driven machines
and create an oxymoron;
a kind of rhythmic melody that syncopates our reflexes,
measuring distance and distinctly abstracting
how we risk our lives going here and there,
with asphalt and rubber, making sonorous
and strangely majestic music,
like a Thelonious Monk composition,
famously strange, lulling, and a magnificent tempest.

In this song, we punctuate time to
the bass of the bus,
the baritone of the eighteen-wheeler,
the soprano of breaks.
These sounds seduce us into daydreams and intimacy,
as the rivers of traffic mark our journey to our plotted
    destination.

At night, flows of red and white light
—depending on a given direction—
become measures of time and possibilities.
Where are we going?
Home?
To a celebration?
To our last minutes here?

Spewing tons of toxins
We travel as friends of speed
and guests of mendacity.
Where are we going?
Will we play there?
Will be pray there?
Where are we going?

Instinctive Ode

— for Castle Street, Worcester and Dennis Brutus

Out near a drunken homeless man,
near a corner where a prostitute keeps count
of what others call time,
there is a rhythm,
beyond greatness and endurance,
something, which does not need to be glorified,
experienced, or cursed slightly.
Something she has no name for, cares to understand,
love, or mother.
Something, which she might even stab,
or throw away as garbage.
Something biological
with no protection from bombs, drugs, or bullets.
Something cellular and molecular,
and not concerned with pride or humility.
A soup of sorts, allied with stars and cosmic histories,
    complicated,
but at the same time so inherently simple
that even elderly residents who have never
learned to wipe themselves or use a toilet
fully understand and even worship,
instinctively knowing they are part of the song,
a part of something, that perhaps cannot be described,
but is close enough to the tapestry
that is the miracle of a single cell developing
into a cat, or a big dog with a wagging tail,
or a human in awe with a newly identified galaxy.

Something, which at its worst
is synonymous with pain, and at its
best,
what some call
God.

Born in rural Mississippi in 1931, Etheridge Knight spent his formative years between there and Kentucky, where his father had moved the family. After dropping out of school at the age of 16, Knight enlisted in the army and served as a medical technician in the Korean War until 1950, when he sustained a serious wound, as well as psychological trauma, which led to his use of morphine and drug addiction. Later convicted of armed robbery, he spent several years in prison. "I died in Korea from a shrapnel wound," he wrote, "and narcotics resurrected me. I died in 1960 from a prison sentence and poetry brought me back to life." Upon his release from prison in 1968, Knight married poet Sonia Sanchez, but the marriage ended two years later, due to his ongoing drug addiction. He would eventually rehabilitate and begin a serious life of poet and teacher. In the years following his first book, *Poems from Prison*, Knight's poetry earned fellowships from the Guggenheim Foundation and the National Endowment for the Arts, and in 1985, the Shelley Memorial Award from the Poetry Society of America, in recognition for his distinguished achievement in poetry. His other books include: *Belly Song and Other Poems* (Broadside Press; Detroit, MI: 1973); *Born of a Woman: New and Selected Poems* (Houghton Mifflin; Boston, MA: 1980); and *The Essential Etheridge Knight* (University of Pittsburgh Press; Pittsburgh, PA: 1986). In 1990, he earned a bachelor's degree in American poetry and criminal justice from Martin Center University in Indianapolis, and taught at the University of Pittsburgh, University of Hartford, and Lincoln University, before he was forced to stop working, due to illness. Knight died from lung cancer in 1991.

Etheridge Knight performed at Noh Place in January 1988, facilitating a poetry workshop, followed by a featured reading.

"Feeling Fucked Up", "Rehabilitation & Treatment in the Prisons of America", "Upon Your Leaving", "He Sees Through Stone", "Prison Graveyard", and "Various Protestations from Various People" from *The Essential Etheridge Knight* by Etheridge Knight, ©1986. Reprinted by permission of the University of Pittsburgh Press.

Rehabilitation & Treatment
in the Prisons of America

The Convict strolled into the prison administration building to get assistance and counseling for his personal problems. Inside the main door were several other doors proclaiming: Doctor, Lawyer, Teacher, Counselor, Therapist, etc. He chose the proper door and was confronted with two more doors: Custody and Treatment. He chose Treatment, went in, and was confronted with two more doors: First Offender and Previous Offender. Again he chose the proper door and was confronted with two *more* doors: Adult and Juvenile. He was an adult, so he walked through that door and ran smack into two *more* doors: Democrat and Republican. He was democrat, so he rushed through that door and ran smack into two *more* doors: Black and White. He was Black, so he rushed—*ran*— through that door—and fell nine stories to the street.

Upon Your Leaving

— for Sonia

Night
and in the warm blackness
your woman smell filled the room
and our rivers flowed together. became one
my love's patterns. our sweat/drenched bellies
made flat cracks as we kissed
like sea waves lapping against the shore
rocks rising and rolling and sliding back.

And
your sighs softly calling my name
became love songs child/woman songs
old as a thousand years new as the few
smiles you released like sacred doves. and I
fell asleep, ashamed of my glow, of my halo, and
ignoring them who waited below
to take you away when the sun rose. . . .

Day
and the sunlight playing in the green leaves
above us fell across your face traced the tears
in your eyes and love patterns in the wet grass.
and as they waited inside in triumphant patience
to take you away I begged you to stay.
"but, etheridge," you said, "i don't know what to do."
and the love patterns shifted and shimmered in your eyes.

And
after they had taken you and gone, the day
turned stark white. bleak. barren like
the nordic landscape. I turned and entered
into the empty house and fell on the floor.
laughing. trying to fill the spaces your love had left.
knowing that we would not remain apart long.
our rivers had flowed together.
we are one.
and are strong.

He Sees Through Stone

He sees through stone
he has the secret eyes
this old black one
who under prison skies
sits pressed by the sun
against the western wall
his pipe between purple gums

the years fall
like overripe plums
bursting red flesh
on the dark earth

his time is not my time
but I have known him
in a time gone

he led me trembling cold
into the dark forest
taught me the secret rites
to make it with a woman
to be true to my brothers
to make my spear drink
the blood of my enemies

now black cats circle him
flash white teeth

snarl at the air
mashing green grass beneath
shining muscles

ears peeling his words
he smiles
he knows
the hunt   the enemy
he has the secret eyes
he sees through stone

Prison Graveyard

The dying sun
slides over the tiger teeth
lying row on row
beneath the high and western wall.

And tonight as the keepers
march in the moonlight
the spirits will rise and fret

And fight because no hymns
were sung to soothe
their journey to eternity,
no mourners stood in solemn stance
and wept;

So the spirits dance
the devil's step, and are kept
from riding the winds to the sea.

Feeling Fucked/Up

Lord she's gone done left me done packed/up and split
and i with no way to make her
come back and everywhere the world is bare
bright bone white   crystal sand glistens
dope death dead dying and jiving drove
her away made her take her laughter and her smiles
and her softness and her midnight sighs—

Fuck Coltrane and music and clouds drifting in the sky
fuck the sea and trees and the sky and birds
and alligators and all the animals that roam the earth
fuck marx and mao fuck fidel and nkrumah and
democracy and communism fuck smack and pot
and red ripe tomatoes fuck joseph fuck mary fuck
god jesus and all the disciples fuck fanon nixon
and malcolm fuck the revolution fuck freedom fuck
the whole muthafucking thing
all i want now is my woman back
so my soul can sing

NOH PLACE

PRESENTS

THE MONDAY NIGHT POETRY WORKSHOP

RAYMOND DUNCAN

EVERY MONDAY AT 7:30 P M

NOH PLACE, 117 Lovell Street, at Maywood

Worcester, Ma. 01602

for information: 753-4914

(CRITIQUE SESSIONS, NOT MERELY READING SESSIONS)

Various Protestations from Various People

Esther say I drink too much.
Mama say pray dont think too much.
My shrink he say I feel too much,
And the cops say I steal too much;
Social Workers say I miss my Daddy too much,
That I dream of driving a Caddy too much.
White folks say I'm lazy and late too much,
Not objective—depend on fate too much.
Philosophers say I wanna BE too much.
Reagan say I talk about me too much,
Singing songs 'bout being free too much.

I say—sing about me being *free* too much?
Say sing about me being *free* too much?

Jacob Knight, folk artist, sculptor and poet, whose birth name was Roger Jaskoviak, was born in Southbridge, Massachusetts in 1938 and grew up in East Brookfield. He graduated from Leicester Junior College, and then moved to Hollywood, California, to become a movie extra, working under the pseudonym of John August. After returning east, he lived in Greenwich Village and worked as a street artist, before eventually making his way back to Massachusetts. His unique style of contemporary folk art drew the attention of collectors. In particular, he became known for his well-researched portraits of Central Massachusetts communities, including the Brookfields, Spencer, Warren and Palmer, which incorporated local legends and history, and were highly regarded for their meticulous brush strokes and astounding detail, artwork that would be published in such journals as *Family Circle, Smithsonian, Yankee Magazine*, and *James Beard's Calendar and Recipe Book*. He also became locally renowned for eclectic found-art sculptures, made largely from items retrieved from the town dump, which populated the yard of his home on Wigwam Road in West Brookfield. Much lesser known as a poet, his writing has yet to be properly collected. Knight died in Worcester in 1994.

Jacob Knight performed his poetry at Noh Place in April 1987, and also during that month contributed art for a group show, "The Painted Poet."

Poems reprinted by kind permission of Pamela Jaskoviak. "The Old Stray Dog" first appeared in *The Worcester Review*.

Lover's Grave

Do not come to my house wearing Red,
for I may take you for an apple or a plum
and eat you.
Then where would you be?
No No No.
Do not stand in my doorway looking pretty,
for I may put you in a vase and keep you
as a wild rose.
Do not come to my house wearing Blue,
No No No,
for I may take you for a Blue Bird and adore you.
Then who would you be?
Do not come to my house dressed in Yellow,
for I might take you as the Sun and adore you.
Then what would you do, to see a naked man?
Do not come to my house wearing Brown,
for I may take you for a Dove or a Doe,
and call you "Dear One."
Do not come to my house wearing Green,
for I might take you for the Wild Witchy Woods
and live within you.
Do not come to my house wearing Black . . .
Never come to my house wearing Black,
for I may haunt you to a Lover's Grave.

The Old Stray Dog

When asked about his name
And, to whom it was
He belonged,
And, was it true
That he was really *lost?*
. . . The old stray dog
Jumped for joy to think
That someone cared . . .
But also shrunk in sadness
That he was found by strangers
Who knew nothing of his past
And took him in . . .
Not knowing that
He pees in corners
And can never stop.

Jacob's Ladder

And he dreamed,
and behold a ladder
set upon the earth
and its top reached to heaven
and behold the angels of God
ascending and descending on it.
                    — Genesis 28:12

In a game called Jacob's Ladder,
Small, flat rectangles of wood
Are strung together with colored ribbons
And flip-flop into a house,
A bird, a man, a lobster, a frog
A butterfly, a bat, a bell,
A whirl-a-gig, a snake,
A mouse trap, all letters of the alphabet.
And in Jacob's hands
Become whole towns
Complete with steeples, buildings,
Factories, fire engines, houses,
Marching bands—all the streets
And all the people.
As October ribbons fall into November
The marks of his ladder
On all the walls still hold brilliant
Rainbow impressions
Of angels frolicking
Down below.

I Call Myself a Painter:
A Portrait of Jacob Knight

— Adapted from a song by Dave Mallet, 1977

I knew a painter in my younger days—
A man who lived with brushes, sticks and stones.
His days were filled with canvas scenes,
Of browns and blues and meadow greens.
And the world just passed by his door
Where he lived, and lived alone . . . .

And he'd come to town
With his old wool hat pulled down,
Surrounded by the dogs that were his friends.
Reading poems with the band
He'd shake a million hands
And sit in this Olde Tavern
'Till his loneliness would end . . . .

And I knew a painter in my reckless days,
Bristle-bearded
And honest were his needs
Sympathetic
Sad Old Elf.
He knew me better than I knew myself!
And the last days of my boyhood in good time
Went to seed.

And long through the night a faded yellow light
Would burn inside the room
Where he would stand
And play the Olde Victrola
And drink his rusty wine

And conduct the Mozart music
With his heart and steady hand.

Still—he could paint a picture
And he could capture life
And no one felt things more than he.

He was never much for roses.
He'd sooner paint the thorns 'cause he'd found
The key to beauty there that no one else
Could see . . .

They might paint the house he lived in
And forget about the room he died in
And sweep away the cobwebs
And the dust off the floor.

Kids will laugh and streams will run.
Young lovers will roll in midnight fun,
Which no one will love more than the one
Who paints the world with such warmth.

And long through the night a faded yellow light
Would burn inside the room
Where he would stand
And play the Olde Victrola
And drink his rusty wine
And conduct his favorite music
With his heart and shaky hand.

Jean Lozoraitis: I was born in City Hospital, Worcester, Massachusetts, second child of Helen and Joseph, raised in Auburn . . . spent a large amount of my childhood singing in an ancient and huge oak tree across the field from my house, called 'The Octopus.' I would spend one Sunday visiting my grandmother who lived on Lake Quinsigamond next to the Lithuanian club, smoking cigarettes in secret with my cousin Mary and eyeing the boys. The alternate Sunday I would visit Pa on the farm, cleaning out cow stalls and skating on frozen ponds in the woods with my sisters, Susan and Helen.

I graduated from Auburn High School in 1968 (Thank you, Mr. Leonard for my love of Spanish, Mrs. Stead for Sir Walter Scott's "The Lady of the Lake" and Mrs. Dorenkamp, who helped me realize I was a poet) . . . graduated from the University of Massachusetts in 1973 (BA, Elementary Education); Fitchburg State College in 1981 (MEd, Bilingual Special Education); Antioch New England Graduate School in 1984 (Waldorf Teacher Training Program); University of Massachusetts in 1992 (EdD, Cultural Diversity and Curriculum Reform). I attended the Atelier House of Assenza Painting in upstate New York, and learned about painting based on the Goethean Color Theory.

I published two poetry books (*LoudcrackSofthearts* and *Down The Longest Road*), wrote, produced and directed a musical (*And the Blues Is Just A Little Headache Now*) and acted in local theatre groups in Boston and Worcester (Todd's Minute Theatre, with Dr. Todd from Worcester State College). I participated in the forming of Noh Place, a uniquely creative and inclusive artists' collective. I enjoy playing, singing and writing music and painting abstract watercolors. I have a husband, Mil, and two sons, Misha and Nikolai. New York has been my home since 1993, but my accent still betrays me.

Poems published with the permission of the author. "En Mexico—Gto." was first published in *LoudcrackSofthearts: the poetry of Jean Lozoraitis* (South End Press, Boston, MA: 1979).

Stories . . .
— Shrewsbury, Mass., circa 1980

Dad said Burt Lancaster
used to go swimming in Lake Quinsigamond . . .
that Burt and Mary Em
had two boys who looked
just like him . . . He said every Spring
the men at White City Amusement Park
tested the roller coaster with sandbags,
then let the kids ride free all morning.

Smiles O'Timmins with one arm and one leg
would climb a 100' tower, light himself afire
and jump into a tank below . . . there were diving horses, too.

And once, The Man Who Wrestled Alligators
lost one of them.
everybody claimed they saw it in the lake,
but the poor thing never made it
past the roller coaster.

Corey's hotdogs cost a nickel,
a pint of ice cream was 15 cents
and a Model-T Ford went for $350.
"Ah, the pleasures of life," says Dad,
"The simple pleasures!"

En Mexico—Gto.

No hay luna esta noche en San Miguel . . .
se fue a los Estados Unidos
en busca de una mejor oportunidad . . .

No hay luna esta noche en San Miguel . . .
Se derritió y aterrizó en un jardin
donde se convertió en un lirio
que un granjero trajo al mercado
para vender por un peso . . .

No hay luna esta noche:
uno de los ninos pensó que era
una pelota, la arrebato del cielo . . .
Y todavia se puede verla
rebotando en las calles
después del atardecer.

There isn't a moon tonight in San Miguel . . .
It went to the United States
For a greater opportunity . . .

There isn't a moon tonight in San Miguel . . .
It melted, fell into a garden
Where it turned into a lily
That a farmer brought to the market
To sell for a peso . . .

There isn't a moon tonight:
One of the children
Thought it was a ball, snatched it from the sky . . .
And you still can see it
bouncing in the streets
After the sun sets.

view from room 7

— circa 1979

Silver milkweed pods blow alongside
the patch of gold hay.
Outside, it's full.
Inside, they keep asking
"When's lunch?"
Second time in two weeks
someone broke the window,
stole the peanuts
and the teacher's Lipton tea.

In the trees, brown thrush
protect their nest . . .
children with coffee bellies
don't grow so soft, come in,
smell like shit
While music lady
toca, toca la viola
free for all to learn—Compliments
of the grumble public
who see welfare
as the reason for inflation
and the poor
as standard deviation.
Outside,
stern faces ride motoras past puberty
into unemployment.
Even pheasants run across the fields
sometimes.

2 dreams

— 1987

I

Some women are spearing fish down by the river.
They ask me why I have trouble believing in God.
I tell them
Death is all around me. I am afraid.
Juan tells me I must have courage.
The Indian man passes a pipe to me.
He says, "We are all here, the living and the dead.
Just ask us for help . . . it is the search that defines you,
only the search . . ."

II

The baby shook the heads of wheat—big,
ripe and golden . . .
Sleek, white llama roamed the farm.
A beautifully colored parrot turned into a snowy white owl
    with a feathery chest.
He said to me—
"You can be whatever you want,
Just be greater than yourself."
I said "I know" . . . then flew away.

Sunday, Feb. 7th

" Jazz in Worcester "

A FESTIVAL BY LOCAL MUSICIANS

**Will be held and sponsored by
Noh Place artists' cooperative
117 Lovell St., Worcester, MA 01603**

featuring the following local artists

12:00 noon	*Dagnello Quartet*
1:00	*Fred Lilienkamp & Guests*
2:00	*Jean Lozoraitis & John Zaganiacz*
3:00	*Dan Stearns & Jim Capone*
4:00	*Heffernan Fortune Quartet*
5:00	*Jane Miller Quintet*

This event was created by Noh Place to show support for our local jazz musicians. Your attendance at this event makes a very loud statement as to how important the local artist community is.

Freedom's Theme

— 1984

I write about people I meet
loneliness I feel
battles that need to be fought.
I write
urging women to make no sacrifice
when it comes to personal power,
about still hungry children in 1984.
nuclear madness blues
being a vegetarian
herbal teas for medicine,
and still say to my soul.
"You got to come up with
Something New! Take them to
Greater Highs, Lower Lows,
Meaner means—nothing less than Supreme . . . !"

I have pondered mysteries in public libraries,
Searched for my soul in confessionals,
Travelled to see if it was in jungle ruins
Or somebody else's culture.

I write about love, death, politics,
Console with possibilities, seduce with words . . .
But I understand that my freedom is at stake,
And though my themes may change,
There is only one I live for.

Origins of Michel Duncan Merle

Born in Paris 1937, woke up at the Akademia Raymond Duncan in the Latin Quarter where my grandparents had created a cultural center featuring theater, music, poetry and crafts such as weaving, letterpress & publishing, silk scarves and wraps decorated with woodblock designs colored by natural dyes and inspired by Greek Mythology as depicted on ancient vases; also the famous Duncan sandals bought by Parisian artists, writers, actors and musicians. Yellow and white posters with giant handcarved letters were hung on the walls of the printshop. The theater featured local singers, poets, vignettes of Greek Tragedies, Raymond's Conferences conducted in French, and the occasional life-drawing session; Chopin pianist, Victor Gille played on the Steinway every Thursday. While Isadora had danced to Classical Orchestras all through Europe and South America, Raymond had by the early twenties settled in Paris for good. He was no longer with his wife, Penelope Sikelianos, who had died of TB during WW I. Penelope had been a pioneer in Greece for her promotion of folk dances, folk crafts, and folk music. Sister of one of Greece's most famous poets, Michel Sikelianos, she soon was welcomed on the lecture circuit. My grandmother Aia, from Latvia, educated at the Sorbonne, taught classes and trained apprentices, managed most of the activities and printed the weekly, *New-Paris-York*. My father, Pierre Merle, had been assistant director and stage designer for the new wave filmmaker, Jean Vigo; after Vigo's death of TB prior to the War, Pierre became music programmer for French radio and stage manager for the Cirque d'Hiver, where clowns, jugglers and acrobats entertained families in Paris. My grandfather, Eugene Merle, had created the satirical newspaper, *le Merle Blanc*. He was a dapper dresser, head of The Baudelaire Society; however, despite his friendship with Clemenceau, France's prime minister, he'd be jailed from time to time: on one such occasion, after my future grandmother's conjugal visit, she later added the days and declared to her husband that she was pregnant with (my father).

America: Christmas 1947 aboard ship, New Years 1948 in New York City.

Two feet of real snow, then to Charlottesville where stepfather Frank Hoskins was finishing MA in English Lit. First day of school in schoolbus, bad-boy is teasing me too much, I had a reflex which propelled my fist toward his nose. Second day in class, teacher says slaves were well treated "back then"; I report to Frank, he and I visit Principal: no, they won't change textbooks. Next two years in Shanx Village, Army camp transformed into housing for ex-soldiers on the GI Bill; Frank is starting PhD at Columbia. At home, he reads from classics to my brother Jean-Pierre and me. I learn English in one year. Frank, who had been a reporter for the *Stars and Stripes*, was a very good teacher. I say to those who complain about immigrants who do not learn English in one year (or more), "How well would you learn Chinese or Hindi or Urdu?" 1950 off to Tucson, Frank is professor at U. of Arizona. I major in Desert Studies. 1955 Frank has defended the PhD, yet is let go despite his considerable contribution to the English Department. Though intolerant of racism Frank accepts a position in the South; my mother is intolerant of his decision (with a Southern mother and a NY-born father, career officer handicapped by Lou Gherig Disease, he did not hate the South though he hated their weaknesses). After the split-up, I did my first year where he taught, East-Carolina College. In my history class the professor says, "The slaves were well taken care of."

....

New York	1956-58	Swiss Bank Corporation, (Foreign Exchange Dept.), Wall Street
	1958-61	Columbia University, BA Cultural Anthropology, Art Minor
	1961-62	" " MA Comparative Education
Texas	1962-64	Fort Hood, drafted as Medic, assigned to Orthopedics, base hospital
New York	1964-66	Social Worker, South Bronx
Mexico	1966-67	Instituto Allende, San Miguel de Allende, MFA Sculpture & Painting
W. Va.	1967-69	West Virginia State College, Instructor of Painting and Figure Drawing
Penn.	1969-71	Pennsylvania State U., PhD Program, Art Education, (ABD)
Worcester	1971-2006	Faculty, Art Dept., Worcester State College (Asst., Associate, full Prof)

Worcester, Mass.

Grove Street Gallery: Co-Founder, curate two or more shows yearly, 15 years; Worcester Artist Group, 7 years; Noh Place; Invented Thing Quartet; Forbidden Poets; Theater Now; Kasner Gooch Multimedia; WCUW-FM: program featuring The Stranger, "Think Tank Tango", 29 years

Poems reprinted with permission from the author.

Alphabet of Refusals

A,B,C   *C:*

I refuse in this Catty voice of mine that Cat-Calls in staCatto rhythms that I Can't Control. I say, "Catch me if you Can! I won't Cater to my better nature: I'll wave this Cat-o-nine-tails in mortal Combat, you ConCupiscent neo-ConCeptualist!"

D:

I refuse through the Dull throb of the Doldrums. The grey Dullness of Doom looms ahead like some Drowsy, Drudging, Dead-Drunk Descent into Dread. I refuse, in this Dream that Drags me Down, and Dare to Drone on and on, Drowning in my self-Doubt, Drop by Drop.

E:

I refuse Effortlessly like an Effervescent vision of Encouragement. I refuse with an Effusive Verve, bent on Endorsing an Empathetic flow of Endorphins. I refuse while Empowering you to Encompass my Elitist views.

ETC ....

Alphabet of the Comforts of Home

B:

My Bedroom is Bathed in Beautiful Begonia Blooms which Beckon me, Begging me to Be a Bouncing Baby Boy again!

C:

Clothes! Of Course, a Cornucopia of Classy Clothes, like Conventional Cutaways Created for Calvin Coolidge, the Cashmere sweaters, but don't Count out the Closet-full of Comfortable Corduroys.

A cut-poem: *from* And if there are other-than-motives I want to know

It was Robert who looked
nuts in rice pudding, that is
I dreamed last night that
Robert has a book about dreams.
He said. "I'm taking my children
to be psychoanalyzed," he
held them hopelessly
and nodded his grayish trees

...

He ran, then
moved about the rooms,
noticed that his hair was ill-prepared
Then became music, a vacuum

...

I dream he is in danger. A miasmic quality
without railings, a bridge that swayed
a deep ravine on a terrifying bridge
within reach of
A long, dangerous trapeze

...

but all Robert had done was
now blamed on remoteness from God

...

when this dream came to me,
Robert's explaining had come
to a stop and then, wound up
with a kind of secret....

Neanderthals:

The Neanderthals
Learn to be Neanderthals
Teach all ways to be

The Neanderthals greet you
Hand you gifts of feathers
Gifts of coats of fur

A cut-poem: These cognitive allegories,
. . . we were insatiable, my poet.

I was apart from all claims of affection.
I used to send my poems to magazines.
Taking care of myself, but
If I could fall in love, it might be with
A determined and resilient . . .
melancholy well-bred
still and impassive
rich and everchanging just about everything.
Being near you, next to you
Your name is . . . . . .
Back in the bedroom I see she is waiting in the wings
a street poet who
was just exhilarating,
and "Frauenliebe und-leben," but with
Five quarts of rhubarb preserves, and
smaller dramas and moments of total chaos.
She said quietly, "I like fistfighting in our sleep."
But her fingers slide to my intensity, directness, and
I pull myself upon the bed and lean
Back against the harp, the piano,
. . . it is never too late for a crime of
poems. They look kind of like poems.

The poet,
Herself the lyrical tremolo,
slowly tore off and ate strips from a
neat square patch of blackearth passion
on a gracious suburban lawn,
said, "I almost missed the figurations, textures, and
theology and style of
Isolated harmonics from a tam-tam beat of uxorious ardor."
She stops moving, opens her eyes,
she hugs me, she breaks into wild arpeggios that throb, throb,
rise more slowly on the celesta, the beginning of
Poulenc's "La Voix Humaine":
"I want you to have my piano when blue aerograms
        —boom —boom
In my head: love, love, love."

GULLIVER Part V
GULLIVER FLIES OFF INTO THE WILD BLUE YONDER

GULLIVER WAS MORE THAN AMAZED BY
AMELIA EARHART'S AIRCRAFT
"SO YOU ARE A PIONEER OF SORTS?," HE ASKED
"OH YES! WOMEN ARE SELDOM SEEN
DOING WHAT I DO . . ."
"AND YES! I HAVE OFTEN THOUGHT THAT
FLYING IS THE LURE OF BEAUTY"
GULLIVER ADMIRED HER POETIC TURN OF MIND
"I MYSELF HAVE OFTEN THOUGHT OF
WRITING ABOUT MY TRAVELS"
THEY WERE FLYING TOWARD SOME CLOUD FORMATIONS—
HE POINTED:
"THOSE CLOUDS ARE AKIN TO THE RUMINANTS
OF THE SERENDIPITY,"
(HE SUSPECTED THAT HE'D MISQUOTED SOMETHING)
"YES, VERY MUCH LIKE THE BUFFALO OF THE
GREAT PLAINS OF AMERICA,"
SHE'D ADDED THAT, REGRETTING THAT SHE'D
NEVER BEEN THERE
AND SO THEY FLEW ABOVE A GREAT HULKING
BAVARIAN PASTRY AND SO TOO THROUGH THE TEETH
OF A FROTHY SAWTOOTH MOUNTAIN AND THEN DODGED
SOME TRUMP TOWERS MARCHING
IN DISARRAY HAVING LANDED ON EACH CLOUD
FORMATION FOR PICNICS
HAVING EXPLORED EACH BIT OF THE VASTNESS OF EARTH'S
CANOPY THEY FINALLY SETTLED DOWN
GENTLY IN A MOUSSE OF THE GARDEN OF EDEN
"LET US NAP HERE TONIGHT AND PARTAKE OF
PILLOW-TALK," GULLIVER SAID—HE WOKE UP TO THE

REALIZATION THAT 'THE QUEST' WAS BECKONING
HE HAD DREAMED OF ADVENTURES NOT REALIZED
SHE AGREED: "BUT PREPARATION IS RIGHTLY
TWO-THIRDS OF AN ADVENTURE"
GULLIVER SUSPECTED SHE HAD DISCOVERED
A FLAW IN HIS MAKE-UP
"OH DON'T FRET," SHE CONSOLED,
"YOUR ADVENTURES ARE YOURS TO SEEK"
SHE PATTED HIS ARM, "COURAGE, MY FRIEND"
HE THOUGHT IT OVER,—
"YOU TOLD ME SOMETHING LAST NIGHT"
"YES, I SAID NO KIND ACTION STOPS WITH ITSELF,"
"ONE KIND ACTION LEADS TO ANOTHER"
GULLIVER WAS DETERMINED TO DO HER A GOOD TURN
THEN REMEMBERED WHAT SHE'D ALSO
TOLD HIM THE NIGHT BEFORE:
"ADVENTURE IS WORTHWHILE IN ITSELF."
HE WANTED TO OFFER HER MORE:
"WHAT EXOTIC TREASURE DO YOU DESIRE?"
"YOU DON'T HAVE TO DO THAT", SHE SMILED,
"JUST WISH ME LUCK"
AND THEY FLEW WEST AND SO THE WHOLE
WIDTH OF THE EARTH WAS PASSING AS THEY
OVERFLEW THE GREAT PYRAMIDS GULLIVER
PRAISED AND PRAISED AMELIA QUIPPED,
"NOT SO FROM HERE, CHUM, SHOW ME A MOUNTAIN"
GULLIVER, WANTING TO PLEASE SAID, "HOW ABOUT
MOUNT ARARAT?" "OK"
AND SO THEY TALKED OF THEIR SPECIAL RELATIONSHIP WITH
TIME AND SPACE.

THE STRANGER MEETS THE GHOST SHADOWS

NOH PLACE

An evening of performance art.....

"A THEATRICAL EXPERIENCE WHICH WILL MAKE YOU WANT TO DANCE"

Lovell Street, at Maywood (off Park Ave)
Worcester, Ma

FRIDAY AND SATURDAY
JUNE 19 & 20, 1987
curtain time: 8:00

with

André Juarez   Michael Lukaszevicz
Brian Jyringi   Charlie Majka
Joyce Kegeles   Michel Duncan Merle

Waiting Room:

Walking to and fro
Pacing back and forth
Humanity sleeps

Walking back and forth
Waiting room crowded with waiters
Everybody wants to walk out

Bill O'Connell lives in the Pioneer Valley in Western Massachusetts with his wife, Robin Marion. A retired social worker, he teaches literature and writing at Greenfield Community College and runs a small handyman business. Bill has published two full-length collections of poetry: *When We Were All Still Alive* (Open Field, 2021) and *Sakonnet Point* (Plinth Books, 2011) and a chapbook, *On the Map to Your Life* (Dytiscid Press, 1992). Website: billoetry.wordpress.com.

Poems reprinted with permission from the author.

Confessional

I am obviously fond of the game
of simple deception learned as a child:
how to avoid pain, the belt, the smack,
by sleight of hand, and later in marriage
and work and with myself,
the halves of the soul arguing, reasoning
in the abyss between the bloom of alcohol
and destruction.
                    Towards
winter now, the dark coming down,
the woodstove lit—autumn
bled out, a certain
reveling in it, what makes us keener
in these heated rooms
deceiving nature, the soul soothed
by the promised stillness of snow, each syllable's
marbled sleight of tongue, the deception
of naming.

America Is Too Busy for Grief

Sunlight through a thundercloud—
    dusk between trees, beyond
        the river
                working from
the ground up.
      I begin to lie to you
again:
    alcohol
is a lie, the bloom
      without petals or scent.

Music saves me, over and over—
    fingers across the keys
        with their own mind.
Nothing is given up—the pond
      reveals nothing, the sky
           keeps its mouth
shut.

What do the dead know
about gravity? a friend says
           the soul unleashed, heading
outward—
      I open my eyes
and the world visits.

At night the stars inside me
firmly fixed, stenciled on
an errant map of the Universe.

Twin Towers

They are like phantom limbs
coming back in the night
before they dissolve—all,
all into fire.

No one imagined except Osama
what could happen.

Even the firemen
bringing their axes
up stairwells to flame.

What could they do? Nothing.
What did they do? Everything.

That day they moved through
the steps of a day. That day
Osama sat and dreamed. Dead now,
dispatched by a Marine.

Still, he remains—
coming back in the night
wounding our grief.

Scratch Dancing

Devil do, devil does—
three lawyers write poems for him.
But when he comes at night,
they dream of money.

Once he came to me, tried to
crawl into my heart.
I grabbed my pillow
and swung at the dark.

This evil's been passed on:
I saw it in a corner
of my grandmother's eye,
next to her faith.

The devil never made a flower,
a poem, never made love.
He moves among the couples
with a cleaver.

But the devil will dance,
will do the fandango,
all night, alone,
with you.

NŌH PLACE

artists co-op
117 Lovell St
Worcester, Ma 01603

CALENDER FOR SEPTEMBER '87

SUNDAY	MONDAY	TUESDAY	WEDNESDAY	THURSDAY	FRIDAY	SATURDAY
		1	2	3 **JIM BARCLAY** Worcester's only licensed street musician. 8:00 P.M.	4	5
6	7	8	9	10 **CRAIG SEMON & CARA-JEAN COSENZA** POETRY FROM THE EXTREME 7:30 P.M.	11	12 **DICK CHASE** Exhibit opening of his paintings 8:00 P.M.
13	14	15	16	17 **T.S. BLACKSTONE** a.k.a. **MIKE LUKASEVICZ** An evening of pugilistic mysticism 8:00 P.M.	18 **DAVID MAJKA** PRESENTS **PSYCHIC BREATHING** 8:30 P.M.	19
20 **BILL O'CONNELL & FRIENDS** Tantalizing rusticity from the jazzhead of Western, MA 4:00 P.M.	21	22	23	24 **CHRISTOPHER GILBERT** 1985 winner of the Walt Whitman award in poetry 7:30 P.M.	25	26
27	28 **ACOUSTIC JAM** bring your instruments and good vibes 8:00 P.M.	29	30			

Jazz Calendar on Back

Blowing Glass

— for my brother Tom

The glass blower
fingers his trumpet,
nimble hands curling neck arched back
sucking in a firestorm
crushing his lungs, heart, blood
pumping as he blows and blows
like Miles, like
Sunday dawn jam cutting solos, blow
blossoming out of blow,
neck craning muscles glistening in the heat flaming
woman bulging from her dress scorched man
bulging also, blowing out like Dizzy
cheeks so sweat-hog foul
his shirt reeks
and the glass breast swells,
is blown—a penis, an eye,
a fist clenching, supple lips,
is the climax, sweet breath
and melting glass
thrust down
into the flames again
before it
cools.

Eve Rifkah was co-founder of Poetry Oasis, Inc. (1998-2012), a non-profit poetry association dedicated to education and promoting local poets. Founder and editor of *DINER*, a literary magazine with a 7-year run. She was the 2021 recipient of the Stanley Kunitz Award. She has run an ongoing writing workshop for 15 years and teaches workshops and classes at WISE (Worcester Institute for Senior Education). She lives in Worcester, MA with her husband, musician, artist, writer Michael Milligan and their cat. She is author of *Dear Suzanne* (WordTech Communications, 2010); *Outcasts: The Penikese Leper Hospital 1905-1921* (Little Pear Press, 2010); *Lost in Sight* (Silver Bow Publishing, 2021); and the chapbooks, *Scar Tissue*, (Finishing Line Press, 2017) and *At the Leprosarium* (2003 winner of the Revelever Chapbook Contest).

Poems from *One Kid, a Telling* (Lachamor Press, 2021), with permission from the author.

Color

The dad's thick fingers smudged
he concentrates   holding tiny
bit of ochre   one hand   sienna other
a TV table holds a box of pastels.

The kid gazes at blue paper
a lady's soft eyes stare back
her hand holds a folded fan.

The kid's fingers itch for color
wants being an artist too.
asks for pastels to use.
The dad says   don't touch.

The dad angry when the kid gets
gifts of kits of paint-by-number
thinks aunts should know better
buy real thing.
Why won't the dad?
the kid wonders.

The ma turns magazine pages
in next room
eating nonpareils.

Night

The kid lies in bed wanting to turn on light
not wanting to see
scurrying things   scurrying things
move so fast

they are there   over the edge
between here and need
the kid holds on tight
wants to make it through
to other side of night

clenches eyes   wills feeling to go away
clicks on light
tiptoes   not wanting to touch floor
sticky floor   rattle and scuttle
floor where dark things live
in bathroom
held breath
and light
and
                        there
against white porcelain
in damp dark stains under faucet

in morning another wet bed
the ma angry
screams

someday the kid thinks
someday enough years stuffed behind
and night will just be night

Green

The kid sees   more green than
the kid ever thought possible
        beyond three-deckers, eyes everywhere.

The kid thinks Monet   like in museum
the kid goes with the dad
place the ma won't go.

The kid don't know arboretum
        not country

climbs twisted tree
            hides in leaves.

Down at bottom   the ma   the dad
dark inside leaf umbrella.

Now sun   blind   eyes close
body in shade
head stuck out on top
        tree a gown
like in fairy tales   goin' to ball
no prince kiss here
        no wand-ed ladies to tap
        and home begone.

The kid stays in green in sun in dark

till the dad calls.

The kid says   want to stay   want home in trees.

Noh Place Artist's Cooperative and The Worcester Artist Group
PRESENT:

The Second Annual
Unusual Tour of Worcester

Saturday, June 3 - Sunday, June 4, 1989

Story

On the seventh day he rested.
For how long, the kid asked,

reading story of how it all began.
It being everything,
earth, sea, wind, birds, man.
It being all tangles
all woes.

For how long? the kid asks again.
Why doesn't he or
maybe she or perhaps it—
what is this thing called god, anyway?
wake up, take notice.
Or did god turn away
try again some other place?

The kid is full of questions
no one wants to answer.

the kid shakes head
returns book to shelf
keeps hoping for
something to make sense
in this forsaken world.

The Bio of Craig Semon

(The sound of constant banging can be heard in the background)
I have workers renovating one of my poems
They're working on knocking down the fourth wall of poetry

Poetry was thrust upon me like a bad porno movie
No matter how much I wash, I still feel dirty
Now, I realize that, in the end, I will enjoy
The Sponge Bath of the Gods

I will fly among the heaven's angels
Piss in the clouds and not begin to worry

In my dreams, my poems rhyme
In my dreams, I have short hair
I wake up. Not only do my poems not rhyme,
The words aren't even spelled right.

Poems reprinted with permission from the author.

Jesus Poem

The Hebrews have been abused
        By the Romans and the Egyptians too
It's time for the King of the Jews
        To save them

Jesus
Jesus

There's a place
        Where life is good

K Mart
K Mart

It's on the right hand,
        the right hand of God

K Mart
K Mart

There's always,
        always a sale

K Mart
K Mart

Atmosphere

It was a dream
It's cute. It's supposed to be the nuance train.
The table stands, just barely,
    with chair close by
It has three legs,
    the chair,
and the table has no
    center
I stand in the center
    of the table
Guard I must, lose I will
    with rose in mouth
    and vase balanced in palm
No Un bel di vedremo
    for me tonight
Give me the Habanera
    White wash the shadows
    on the walls
    and accent my aura
I don't have voice
    but I do have vanity
If you stretch someone's
    intestines as far as you
    could, you'd probably
    get a room that looks
    similar to this

Fully furnished and the smell
    of the appendicitis
    nurturing the Caesarean
    appetite
I wait for the Habanera
Now that is atmosphere.

Sylvia Plath and the bees

Pull out the eyes of magenta from the sockets
And put bees in their place
Look back at everybody with bee's eyes,
Bee's bodies as eyes
And maybe they will begin to understand,
To stop understanding

Fuck all the men
They are not worthy of the woman
They are not worthy of the woman with bee's eyes
They are not worthy of the bees

Their little funny bodies,
Their little moving bodies have become Sylvia's eyes
With multiple stingers that look inside herself

She was the beauty queen
That saw the world with the honey of her eyes
Her brain was like a beehive
With all her fathers, all her husbands, buzzing

Honey drenched laughter, pollenated wedlock
Wings, clipped, life unearned beyond tomorrow

Skin-thin lampshades cast the dimmest shadows
Human drum skins create the hollowest beat
Skin on aching bones and tired muscle
Are just covering
For a soul I wish to keep

They tried to make Sylvia happy
By making themselves happy
Worshiping the ground she bleeds on
The buzzing is the sound of insanity flying (away)

A Poem to Piss On

In my tears are angels, drowning, gasping for breath
The Lindbergh Baby and the Christ Child
attended college together

       My aim is covered in silk
       Only translations of you can help me
          see the future

I am the vulnerable lover of madness
Everything I love turns to sadness

There are no sexual dynamos left in the world
It's as if I have stumbled on the evolutionary scale of cellulite

       Come to me Kiki
       Let me cut your eye
       And place it on a triste
       Perchance the pendulum
          shall ring true
       I never loved you

You are an extension of death
And this evening has become a night of the ugly

See the Bohos
See the Bohos and their friends
Say Hi to the Bohos
Wave to the Bohos

Art is an infection, an infection on the penis
Some people get it, others like to look at it

Where in the world can I find
a girl named Kiki in
such short notice

ĨŌH PLACe

Absolutely New!

Stephen Anthony Campiglio

One Morning's Face

I pour the milk
And watch it
Pierce the dark
Face of coffee
In my cup.

At first
An arrow shooting
Light into the world,

Then an innocent purity
Lost in poison,

The the poison itself
Coiling at the bottom
Of the cup
To strike
At the face
Less than dark.

Then it is just coffee.

Slick Wadsworth

Haiku:

The looping rope stops.
A young calf fears
    certain death.
Dad says, "good throw son."

*

The die has been cast.
Martians do not worship God.
They bowl Tuesday night.

___

also: BOTTLENECK GUITAR

FLAT JOKES

and more!

*COFFEE*HOUSE*

THUR   APRIL 9th   7:30 pm

NOH PLACE ARTISTS' COOP

119 MAYWOOD ST. WORCESTER

Hear my cries. Feel my agony.

Once, I went out into my backyard and noticed a tree.
   The tree resembled knowledge and the backyard, logic.
   When I decided to build a playhouse in the tree, my mother
      called me in for supper.

I love her.
I'll never forgive her.

Jeff Wadsworth is a well-known guitarist who has been playing in the MA/CT area for upwards of 50 years! Around 1978 he started writing poetry and eventually became interested in Haiku. After studying the form and researching its history, his poet friends urged him to read his Haiku at coffee houses and other events. Since he always thought of himself as a musician first, he was surprised to find that people enjoyed his Haiku. He became known for what he called "Country/Western Haiku," which are poems based on situations found in the Old West. Another interesting twist in his life, which also led to writing, took place in the early 2000s. Jeff owned a golf pro shop and specialized in custom golf club building and repair. The local Hartford Connecticut area newspapers published a few articles about him in their sports sections. He was also a well known golf instructor, and wrote a few articles based on hot topics in the golf world for the sports departments of local newspapers. Jeff hasn't done much writing recently, but continues to play guitar regularly in the Wicked Biscuit band, based in Monson, MA.

Poems reprinted with permission from the author.

*

Cold growing shadows
Goose grey in twilight splendor
Chills run up my spine

*

Trembling with anger
Small child scuffling with elder
Tiny fist shaking

*

Pink clouds to the east
Dusting the sky with color
The storm approaches

*

A lonely line camp
A cowboy's life in winter
The cows look bitter

*

Oh those stupid cows
Although the lightning scares them
They still taste real good

*

The looping rope stops
A young calf fears certain death
Dad says good throw son

*

The prairie whispers
Don't move, prairie dogs ahead
Horses should listen

David Williams was born in Maine, but has spent most of his life in Massachusetts. He has a BA from Hampshire College in Amherst, MA and a Master of Arts in Teaching from the School for International Training in Brattleboro, VT. Over the years, he has taught English as a Second Language to both children and adults. More recently, he taught writing at Wheaton College. Some of his poetry reflects his work with immigrants and refugees. His grandparents were immigrants from Lebanon. Williams is the author of two poetry collections, *Traveling Mercies* (Alice James Books, 1993) and *Far Sides of the Only World* (Carolina Wren Press, 2004). Hs poems have appeared widely in journals and anthologies throughout the years.

Poems reprinted with permission from the author.

Coes Pond

— 1976

With that boat on your back,
you look like a crucified
juggler, or maybe a hermit crab
who can't find a shell that fits. Anyway,
a man with a back for honest work.
I row out. You untangle lines
and clip on iridescent spinners
that half-shield a trinity of hooks.
I'm too lost to find much holy
anywhere famous. Coes Pond,
Worcester, Massachusetts—
we can see the expressway.
The boat drifts near the weeds.
If you see a water strider disappear,
there are fish below. Meanwhile
we just cast and reel in,
cast and reel in,
hoping for more than a lost face
to rise to the surface.
Storm clouds mass.
I linger at the oars,
admiring the iridescence
of heaven at dusk.
Rain draws fish.
The water bears us up.

Still Baking

decades later, still baking,
now in Blessed Sacrament Hall,

the longest war still burning,
no end in sight,

loaves still rising by an invisible
order that lets us breathe,

our parents gone,
our children grown,

new gaps between
thought and word

now part of the story
like rests in a song,

the old themes sometimes
hard to hear,

an inverted bassline,
perhaps, a harmony

by which a new
melody belongs

A Barn-raising in the Wake

Overlook Farm, Heifer Project International
Rutland, Massachusetts, September 22, 2001

Remembering lowering
coffins we pass

slings beneath
dense posts, dense beams

the carpenter signed
precisely with mortise

and tenon (last night's
rain in the hollows)

and left us unskilled
amateurs, love, to

lift, haul, fit,
then tap together,

and peg by lumber's
give and tough grain,

and raise into
a barn frame,

square and plumb
beneath reeling stars.

Palm to Palm: Conscientious Objections

Glance sideways—the dead
still present, still lost.

Monks float upriver—flares and live rounds
from both banks—hauling rice

for cut off villages. Mothers hold out
soon-to-be orphans to the boats.

My daughter hears her daddy refused to fight
and wants to know the whole story.

Then how to explain my cousin who went
and never talks about Tet?

Or my true witness before the draft board,
a Marine, retired, a hawk?

Or those who overcame the Pacific unarmed
to shield children with more than breath?

Relate lotteries, privileges, prisons,
oblivions, exiles, self-immolations?

Once I said no—not much, but windblown
seeds can grow into a windbreak.

✻

Listening now to Kim, Linh, Tran
right here where I live—

their eyes still searching empty sea
for pirates or landfall—a gesture

they save reaches me; palms raised
touch memory, recognition, one body.

CPSIA information can be obtained
at www.ICGtesting.com
Printed in the USA
BVHW041445130922
646898BV00005B/223